Sticky Situations
And Lifestyle
Complications

A Poetic Prelude

By Raynice Starr

Sticky Situations
And Lifestyle
Complications
A Poetic Prelude

For Permission Requests:

Starr Media, Inc.
P.O Box 44031
Muskegon, MI 49444

www.raynicestarr.com

ISBN-10: 1-947195-02-6
ISBN-13: 978-1-947195-02-8

DEDICATION

I dedicate this poem book to everyone who supported and inspired me during the time of writing. Those include my brother, Michael Starr, children, friends, family, loved ones, and grandchildren.

I give a special dedication to my dad, Benny Clark. He was the greatest father in the world! He gave me so much wisdom to live by. He was my best friend. He passed away on March 5, 2007, in my arms. I love you dad.

I also give a special dedication to my beloved son Anthony Fareed Lamb. He was called home to Heaven on September 11, 2016. Rest in peace son. I love you.

Sincerely,

Raynice Starr

TABLE OF CONTENTS

STICKY SITUATIONS, A Poetic Prelude

TABLE OF CONTENTS

TABLE OF CONTENTS

LIFESTYLE COMPLICATION

Sticky Situations
And Lifestyle
Complications

A Poetic Prelude

A Poetic Prelude to a book, that will encourage
you to look at the difficult times in your life, so
you may gain wisdom and understanding...to
help you reduce your strife.

INTRODUCTION

Life can sometimes bring you into situations that may be overwhelming. There are reasons that we encounter hard times in life. Sometimes it's because of something we did. Additional times, it's due to our lack of wisdom to prevent certain situations. Other times, it's a spiritual trial that we must endure. No matter what the situation, it's imperative to understand the underlying reason so you can grow from the experience.

Everything happens for a reason. In ancient Hebrew writings, there were no correlating phrases for the word, coincidence. As a result, the word coincidence was not an understood form of language. Everything in life had meaning. There was a reason that certain things happened. In past societies, people sought out wisdom to determine why a situation occurred.

However, in our fast paced society today, people are impatient with the meaning of things. If we do not immediately understand or comprehend it, we write it off as a coincidence. And, coincidently we continue to go through the same sticky situations over and over again, not understanding why situations are occurring in our lives.

There is a season and a reason for everything in life. Life is a journey. We must strive to understand our paths so that we can assist others on their paths. It is our legacy and duty to help others in their lives.

We are all called to be teachers, whether we desire to be teachers or not. We teach our family, children, friends, associates, and society by the way we behave and respond to issues of life.

What lessons are others learning from our lives? Will they learn lessons that they can model in their own lives? I will assist you in understanding why you are encountering situations in life. As a mother who disciplines her children, when they go astray, my words may be hard sometimes, but they will help you to identify issues in your own life. They will inspire you to take an inward look at what issues are affecting your life emotionally, spiritually, financially, and physically.

As a spiritual lifestyle coach who desires you to win in life, my words will sometimes offend you. However, they will offend you to good works. The poems and short stories will speak to your situation and help you learn where you could grow in wisdom and understanding.

You will begin to expand in your life because you understand what to do and what not to do in certain situations. You will be catapulted to the next level of life, because your wisdom and understanding will cause you to handle situations that are higher than where you are. As you become whole in your soul, your life will manifest the wholeness that is within you. You will live a life of consistent victories in every situation.

In order to go to the next level in life, there must be training. Training is not always easy and fun. However, it will reap a wealth of benefits for your future. Continue to be trained, so you can understand and learn from every situation you encounter. Be made whole in your soul!

STICKY SITUATIONS

A POETIC PRELUDE

STICKY SITUATION

One day, one of my many daughters came to me
and asked, "Mama, what would you do if you were
pregnant and didn't know who was the father of your
baby?

I responded, "I don't know". She then stated, "You
don't know what you would do?" "I thought you knew
a lot about relationships"

My Daughter... there are some things in life, that I
don't know, because there are some questions that I
will never have to ask myself, like...

If I took a drug test, would I fail?
If I went to jail, could I post bail?
And, if I got pregnant, would I know who's the father?
Questions like those I don't even bother.

You see, I have learned to not place myself
in a certain position
by asking the right questions
before the condition.

There are some issues in life
you should never have in the first place.

Because after the fact
they are hard to erase.

So protect and cover yourself
with all dedication.

Before you find yourself in a...

Sticky Situation

Rest For A Weary Man

Dear Ladies:

In all of your power

do everything you can

to provide rest

for a weary man.

GET YOUR HOUSE IN ORDER

Married Ladies:

Are you a wife or are you a knife?
Do you bring increase to his life?

Do you build up
or do you cut up?

Do you keep talking
or do you shut up?

A wise woman builds up her house,
while a foolish woman tears hers down.

A foolish woman wears an attitude
while a wise woman wears a crown.

Be mindful of my words
before you find yourself hiring a lawyer.

The primary purpose of your marriage
is to get your house in order.

You Can't Raise A Man

Single Ladies:

Are you weary about your man
because he still lives with his mama?

Are you tired of all the pain
he puts you through
and all the drama?

There are real men who are mature
and who will aim to please.

They will create a world of fulfillment
and your life will be at ease.

So if you're really upset
about your relationship complications,

know that you can't raise a man
but you can raise your expectations...

Expect more.
Kick him out the door.
Recognize what a real man is for.

If You Want What You Want

If you want what you want
then why not go get it?
But don't be dismayed
when you end up with it.

If you want what you want
don't take the time praying.
What difference does it make
in what God is saying?

When God told you "Don't",
obeying Him...You won't.
Because you're too busy
chasing after want.

Not planting any seeds
towards what your soul needs.
You run after flesh
and all that it feeds.

You disobey God's Word
and what you have heard
mocking all of His prophets
calling them weird and absurb.

If you want what you want
regardless of the cost,
can't come running back to God
when your soul you have lost.

SIDE CHIC

Does he call you one hour
before asking you out on a date?
When he shows up
is he three hours late?

Now it's no longer eight
but closer to eleven.
Nothing good is going on
at that time under heaven.

If you're willing to give,
he's happy to take.
He showed you a little attention.
Now isn't that great!

No strings attached!
He accomplished his plan.
But now you are thinking
that he's your man.

So you call him every day
but he doesn't answer your calls!
Doesn't he even care
about you at all?

You're finally relieved!
He called you back!
But a little disappointed
he wants to jump in the sack.

So you give in thinking
he will surely love you.
But now he's harder to reach.
You don't know what to do!

You feel victimized, and used,
and very upset at him.
Not recognizing that
it is you who are letting him.

If you don't wanna be a victim
you better recognize quick.
This man has made
you his side chic.

Don't accept every behavior.
Don't reach out and grab it.
Don't get in the habit
of being his "silly rabbit".

Recognize early
he wants a chic on the side.
And don't give him the time of day.
Maintain your pride.

Side Chic

Little Patch Of Grey

Little Patch of Grey
why must you plan to stay?
No matter what I do to you
you're back the next day.

Little Patch of Grey
why won't you let me be?
You make it very difficult
to look like I'm twenty-three!

When people compliment me on my hair
they will always say,
"Your color's very beautiful,
but you missed
a little patch of grey".

No matter how determined I am
to try and hide my age.
You're more determined
to let them know
I'm almost a sage!

I cut you, I dye you, I pull you, I fry you.
I cover you with shoe polish
and even with black makeup.
There's something about our relationship
that you won't let us break up!

Every night before I go to bed
I try to pluck you from my head
but it seems you come back
twice as strong
as soon as I wake up!

Little Patch of Grey
you must have a mind
of your own.

It's something about
who you are
that won't leave me alone!

No matter what I do
I can't seem to erase you.
So maybe it's about the time
for me to just embrace you.

DREAM KILLERS

There are people in your life
that compliment your desires, goals, and dreams.

Then there are people in your life
that bring death to your dreams.

It is your responsibility to recognize those
who are hindering your next season.

Your dream requires an acknowledgement
of the wrong people in your life.

Once you identify them,
you must purge the ones that
bring devastation to your dream revelation.

Dream Killers

Just Say No To A PPO

My Dear Young Lady,

What is it about your relationship
that you won't let him break up?

Although you fight and argue all day long,
you insist he makes up.

Forcing him to love you
with your manipulative ways
even trying to get knocked up.

If you don't stop this bizarre behavior
it may just get you locked up.

Just Say No To A PPO

SOUL TIES

Some relationships in life
are only meant to be seasonal.

They accomplished what you needed
at that time in your life.

But in your next season as you grow
you know they can't go.

So release them now
and forever hold your peace...

Soul Ties

THE WEIGHT IS OVER

Dear Single Ladies:

Have you ever had a certain situation?
You feel your weight has caused
romantic complications?

You don't receive many social invitations?
Your appearance has an
effect on your relations?

If you lost a little weight
maybe then you'd get a date.

What about the weight that's in your heart?
Perhaps losing that is smart.

Ridding external weight and saggage
but your heart is full of baggage.

You think that man refuses to marry
cause of the extra pounds you carry.

Although getting healthy
would be really smart.

You must consider weight
that's also in your heart.

Let Jesus heal your soul
and only then will you be whole...

enough to begin a
rewarding brand new start.

WAKE UP ADAM!

Wake up Adam!
Take care of your garden!
before all the hearts
around you have hardened!

Wake up Adam!
While it's yet day,
the time is at hand
and you're sleeping away!

As you're asleep,
your workers all play.
Your garden is in
such disarray.

You toss and you turn
with great depression
not recognizing it's you
holding up your progression.

Your animals run wild.
Your garden's unkept.
Your grass has grown high
because you have slept.

And while you are sleeping
the Serpent is creeping.
Eve is uncovered
because you're not keeping.

You sleep and you slumber,
expecting Eve to wait.
But when you get up
it might be too late!

Wake up Adam!
Get on with your life!
Before you discover
that you have no wife!

If you don't get up
and take care of yourself
you'll find that Eve's gone
to be somewhere else...

Fairy Tale Ending

You say that you
wanna go steady?
But are you really sure
that you are ready?

You say you want a man
that looks like a sex object
but in return,
he will get
a major project!

Your house is nasty.
You can't cook toast.
And just the other day
you burned up a roast!

Your kids are out of order.
Your attitude's bad.
Every time someone sees you
it seems like you're mad.

You got three baby daddies
working on number four.
Number two busted your door.
Need I say more?

Like attracts Like
What signals are you sending?
Will they produce a happy ending?

Will you have a story
like a beautiful fairy tale?
Or a story full of drama
straight out of hell.

You may have had a rough start
but it's not the end of your story.
Give it to Jesus,
and give God the glory!

As you focus on Jesus
and not on your trouble.
He will give you a blessing
a portion that's double!

He'll clean up your mess
and reduce your strife
so you can become
a suitable wife.

And then you'll be healthy
and it won't be alarming
that you will attract
your perfect Prince Charming.

Fairy Tale Ending

No Means No

When they tell you NO
have the strength to let it go.
If they come back to you
then you know that it was true.

If they go astray
God has better anyway.
If they can't make up their mind
help them out by leaving them behind.

God is teaching you a valuable lesson.
Learn how to properly handle rejection.

It doesn't matter what another will do.
You will still have peace within you.

You will respond right every time.
You won't let others make you lose your mind.

Even though, NO means NO,
it doesn't have to mean that you can't go.

You just gotta take another direction.
Take some time for a little correction.

Then go a different way
and you're sure to get there some day!

When you learn how to
respond right to NO,
there's no place on earth
that you can't go.

No Means No

A Taste For Holiness

I inspire you to be the higher you.

God is transforming your desire

Changing what you admire.

So that your soul will acquire...

A Taste For Holiness

THE THIRST IS REAL

Dear Single Lady,

Are you wining and pining
for his affection?
But all you receive
is his rejection?

Are you moaning and groaning
for that man's love?
Giving him more of your attention
than God above?

There's a Spiritual Law
every woman should be learning.
It's God's divine order
for that man to be yearning.

God instructed the man
to take authority in his life.
And, God promised him favor
if he found a wife.

So he takes his job seriously
and goes on his way
searching and seeking
for the perfect wife someday.

I'm gonna tell you a secret.
And I must keep it real.
That man chooses his wife
by how she makes him feel.

If he's not longing for you
take a step back.
Don't wine, don't pine,
or complain of your lack.

The thirst will make it worst.
You must put God first.
He'll rain His Spirit down to quench it,
pouring rain to wet and drench it.

Then the perfect man will know
your satisfaction overflows.
And, he'll desire what's in your life
choosing you to be his wife.

UNREALISTIC EXPECTATIONS

When you have
unrealistic expectations
you create all sorts of
major complications.

You make assumptions
due to lack of information.
And take offense
when you don't know
the situation.

Fine tune your skill
of personal communication.
Then, you will gain
the proper revelation.

Everything Is Working For Your Good

If things are looking kind of odd
still know that He is God.

He promised you a dream
and sometimes it doesn't seem...
like your dream is going to last
or your desires will come to pass.

Pray and believe
then you will know
that in time
your dream will show.

Things will work out just as they should...

Everything Is Working For Your Good

THE SPIRITUAL LAWS OF ATTRACTION

In order to find love
and complete satisfaction
you must learn to obey
the Spiritual Laws of Attraction.

There's a Law of Attraction
to know, you should choose.
The one with the greatest investment
is the one with the greatest to lose.

There's a Law of Attraction
that ladies must not shun.
The harder you chase men
the faster they will run.

There's a Law of Attraction
you didn't get in class.
The quicker you rush love
the shorter it will last.

There's a Law of Attraction
women shouldn't leave on the shelf.
Men will only choose to love you
the same level you love yourself.

There's a Law of Attraction
that tells a secret about love.
The easier they are to get
the harder they are to get rid of.

There's a Law of Attraction
I hope ladies will find.

The more you cover your body
the more he's attracted to your mind.

There's a Law of Attraction
that has not been told.
You must Spit Out the one
who runs Hot and Cold.

There's a Law of Attraction
that's very real.
The sooner women have sex
the lesser men will feel.

There's a Law of Attraction
that everyone should know.
The one with the greatest investment
is the last one to let go.

There's a Law of Attraction
that men should not shove.
A prudent woman will only receive you
when she can trust you with her love.

There's a Law of Attraction
that's fairly known.
Some folks don't recognize a Good Thing
until a Good Thing is gone.

There's a Law of Attraction
that women should not lose.
The one who's easy to sleep with
is the one he won't choose.

There's a Law of Attraction
that might blow some man's mind.
A man must search for a wife
before he will find.

There's a Law of Attraction
that must be addressed.
Because women chase so hard
men have learned to chase less.

There's a Law of Attraction
that reduces strife.
What you fail to celebrate
will exit your life...

The Spiritual Laws Of Attraction

KEEP IT MOVING

Single Ladies:

Did he say...

in order for him
to be with you
you must first
jump through his hoops?

You must first
move to his town?
You must first
lose fifty pounds?

Whether fat or
whether skinny
whether near or
whether far

the number of men
are very many
who will accept you
as you are.

Men who require stipulations
have unrealistic expectations.

If you must first
do all of that
you should leave him
where he's at...

Keep It Moving

Make The Right Choice

Single Ladies:

Choose the one who
sees the best in you
when everyone else only
sees the worst in you.

Choose the one who will
give you protection
who will love and honor,
and give you spiritual correction.

Choose the one who will
increase your life
who will desire to make you
a suitable wife.

Who will cherish your love
who will show you he cares
who will be by your side
who will calm all your fears.

It sometimes can be difficult
with so many choices
while listening and deciphering
so many voices.

But the voice of the Lord
will give you direction.
He will lead you and guide you
to your best selection.

And, when you make up your mind
then you will know
the perfect plan of God
and the way you should go.

I declare I will...

Make The Right Choice

Be Encouraged

Are you going through storms, trials,
and tribulations?

Don't stress about your mess.
It's only a test.

God's killing your flesh.
So you can be blessed.

Be Encouraged

THE LAW OF RECOGNITION

You have ears
but you hear not.

You have eyes
but you see not.

Everything that you ever wanted
is already in your life
awaiting your recognition of it.

There is something in your life
that you are not hearing or seeing
and it's costing you.

Will you open your ears and hear?
Will you open your eyes and see?

Until you recognize,
you will pay the price.

The Law Of Recognition

The Recognition Of A Good Man

Single Ladies:

Desire a man who loves
and adores you.
A man that won't put
other women before you.

Who will be by your side
even when you disagree.

Won't take up for your opposition
when he doesn't see...
your point of view...

He will still trust you.
And, know that your heart
is loving and true.

He will think that you're the best,
better than all the rest.

He won't take pleasure
in your enemies
trying to expose your mess.

He would offer you encouragement
and would simply be sweet.

Ensuring that you know
that you would never ever meet
another that's so kind,
supportive, and strong.

A Good Man that would cover you
from all harm and wrong.

If you find that kind of man
be sure to hold on.

Don't let him go,
because you will know
your life would be blessed
and your happiness would flow.

LOVE REGARDLESS

Have you ever had
a certain situation?
Others trying to
ruin your reputation?

You hear them with
their negative conversation?
And know that they
reject your celebration?

How do you respond
to their nasty words?
When they have no proof
of what they heard?

They accuse you of your
motives and what's inside,
when their own actions and
motives they try to hide.

They mimic you
but reject who you are,
trying to diffuse
your shining star.

Making sure that others
will only see
their constant chants
of negativity.

They hate you with no cause.
They despise your every move.

You ponder in your heart
what do they have to prove?

But then you recognize
that it's only a test.
God's developing you
to be your very best.

He's strengthening your character
to Love Regardless...

To pray for your enemies
when they give you stress.
And to cover them with love
as they expose mess.

Love Regardless

Speaking To My Past

I'm a new woman
and I know that I've closed the door.
I just need more...

I'm a new woman
and I know that I've told you NO!
I must let go.

I'm a new woman
and I can't look back and cause God strife.
Remember Lot's wife?

I'm a new woman
and I know that we had a blast
but I'm afraid it cannot last...

Speaking To My Past

THE SEED OF LOVE

True love is like a seed.
It grows with water, fertilizer, and time.

Continue to water your seed
with words of encouragement.
Fertilize your seed
with acts of kindness.

And in time, watch your seed grow
like a tree planted by the rivers of water
that brings forth its fruit in due season.
Its leaf will not wither.
And whatsoever you do will prosper.

The Seed Of Love

THE LAW OF HONOR

There used to be a time
that I loved to fight.
Always arguing, proving
I was right.

But then God sat me down
for a little conversation.
He gave me insight and
a little revelation.

He told me that my life
was a continuous downer
because it was I
who chose not to honor.

He said that I
was a "rebel without a cause".
He made me take the time
to step back and pause.

So I would know
why I had so much strife.
It was simply because...
I didn't honor others in my life.

Honor your mother and father
for more days on the Earth.
Be sure to honor yourself
to increase your self worth.

Honor your pastor
for spiritual protection.

Honor your teacher
for educational reflection.

Honor your husband
and honor your wife.
Honor the Lord
for eternal life.

There's something about honor
that has such a sweet flavor.

When you choose to honor
you can then savor
the aroma of blessings
and continuous favor.

The Law Of Honor

TAKE A SECOND LOOK

In relationships
there are two perspectives to every story.
There are two sides to every fence.

Are you absolutely sure
that you are reading
the information correctly?

Come to the other side of the fence.
Your back was turned to your answer before,
but now your answer will be right before your eyes.

What will you see on the other side of the fence?
A different point of view.

Take A Second Look

JUST BE YOURSELF

Single Ladies:

In order to attract
your perfect Boo
to yourself,
you must be true

Don't be disingenuous
to him and yourself
by acting like somebody else.

Although men are simple
with communications
they are discerning
when it comes to relations.

They may not say much
but they can see
your lack of individuality.

They choose "The One"
by what they see inside.

They'll know there's something
that you're trying to hide.

So don't dishonor
who God made you at birth
by diminishing your self worth...

Just Be Yourself

JESUS

What's wrong Broken One?
Has the Enemy vexed your soul?
He has caused mayhem
on the battlefields of life.

He is the Deceiver.
His primary purpose is
to make you believe a lie
rather than the truth.

He will crawl into your mind
speak to your imagination
and cause you to feel that
you will not succeed
or you will not receive
the desires of your heart.

You will recognize him
because he will speak against
the will of God for your life.

He will cause you to be weary,
heavy burdened, hard yoked, and tired.

I know a place
where there is healing for your soul.

There is a Balm in Gilead.
It will ease your pain,
sooth your weary mind,
and restore your soul.

Now that you feel better, COME.
Come and drink from the Rivers of Living Water.
You will never thirst again.
They are like a cool spring that
will satisfy your every desire.

You're stronger, you're better,
and your thirst is filled.
You have had a long day.

Now follow me.
I will help you find rest for your soul.
I will take you to a Person.
He will give you rest.
For His yoke is easy and His burden is light.

JESUS

MAKE UP YOUR MIND

You're happy and you're sad,
glad, then you're mad.

You're up and you're down,
a smile, then a frown.

Didn't you know
that God is not the author of confusion?

And a double minded man
is unstable in all his ways.

Make Up Your Mind

Beauty Is Only Skin Deep

Men:

Why did you choose her?
Did you say it's because she's fine, with a cute shape?

But she's angry, bitter, mean, argumentative,
always accusing, with a negative attitude,
and a nasty disposition.

You say you're going to reason with her?
But she is so shallow.

How can you reason with a person who
does not have the depth to look within,
to recognize their shortcomings,
to make a positive change?

Didn't you know that beauty doesn't last always?
What are you gonna do when that "brick house"
turns into a "block house"?

Beauty is only skin deep,
but ugly is to the bone.

Make The Right Choice

THE NEW FACE OF FORTY

Being over forty is amazing
and the best years of my life!
My understanding is much deeper.
I encounter a lot less strife.

My body's not as tight.
I've enlarged in a few spaces.
But I don't mind
because my curves are
still in the right places.

I have a lot more confidence.
I care less what people say.
When I decide to marry again,
I'll make a beautiful wife someday!

I've gained a sense of freedom.
I've come into my own.
I have very little debt
and my children are all grown.

Twenty years ago,
I didn't have a clue of
the things that I know now.

Ask me what I feel
about being over forty?
All I can say is wow!

THERE IS A BALM IN GILEAD

Ladies:

To a man, life is a battle,
the battle of knowing whether
he is living his life fully.

Is he going in the right direction,
living his highest vision,
or just wasting his time.

On the battlefield of life,
sometimes men get broken,
hurt, wounded, and grow weary.

When he comes
back off the feld
into the camp,
we must be his
balm in Gilead.

Become his lubricating salve,
an anointed ointment,
that dissolves his pain,
eases his weary mind,
and heals his wounds.

Then we won't have to wonder,
during his war on life,
"Where's this relationship going?"

We will have no need to pressure him
on the status of our relationship.
We will already know.

THE LAW OF PURSUIT

Dear Men:

Did you say that you want it?
Your pursuit displays your passion.
And you do not qualify to possess
what you fail to pursue.

If you fail to obtain it
you cannot gain it.

If you don't go get it
you won't end up with it.

If you will not grab it
you shall not have it.

If you don't retrieve it
you won't receive it.

If you fail to seize it
God won't release it.

If you don't pursue it
you won't subdue it.

Didn't you know that
it wouldn't fall in your lap?

Then don't be disturbed
when it's not yours...

THIRSTY CHIC

Dear Single Man:

Typically, when a chic is thirsty
she is usually drinking out of
more than one cup.

The Character Of A Man

Does he love you and you know it?
Is he not too proud to show it?

Does he aim to please you?
Promises never to leave you?

Did you get his love letter
encouraging you to be better?

Does he pray to our God above
to cover you with His love?

Are you confident he will stay
until your dying day?

Does he speak increase in your life
desiring you to be his wife?

Does he disregard your past
knowing the future is what will last?

Will he be there until the end
through all thick and thin?

It is that man you should choose
and never want to lose.

Hold on to him real tight
and always treat him right.

Love him and let him know
that you will never let him go.

Be there by his side
on this crazy rollercoaster ride.

Respect him and keep him near
to ease away the fear.

Know that he will be the best
better than all the rest.

Inside every man is a way that he operates.
Some are strong, some sweet, some talk, some don't.

Some are sensitive, some are angry,
some will, and some won't.

You must determine what's best for you.
You must choose the right plan.

And if the perfect one finds you
decide in your heart
for him, you will do all you can.

The Character Of A Man

HOLINESS IS THE NEW SEXY

Do you want to attract the right date?
Become what you desire in a mate.
Holiness is the new sexy!

Pull up those clothes!
Uncurl those toes!
Holiness is the new sexy!

Don't take everybody for a ride in your car.
You're getting too many miles because
you're going to far.
Holiness is the new sexy!

Cover your chest!
Bring down that dress!
Holiness is the new sexy!

Don't be hard to get.
Be hard to sleep with.
Holiness is the new sexy!

Don't let everybody see your show.
Only allow the one who pays the price to go.
Holiness is the new sexy!

Holiness will attract what God has in mind.
He wll bring to you, your equal,
someone who's your kind.

Holiness! Holiness! Holiness!
Holiness is the new sexy!

THE KNOWLEDGE OF LOVE

Ladies:

Do you know if he loves you?
Well, if he loved you
he would never humiliate you
in front of others.

He would confess before his brothers
that you're the one he'd choose
and never want to lose.

He would live a life that doesn't offend you.
His words would always commend you
of the joy you bring to his life
desiring you to be his wife.

He would withstand sexual temptation
just to receive the manifestation
the manifestation of your love
that he confessed to God above.

You would never have to second guess
that your life wouldn't be a mess.
You would have confidence in knowing
that his love is overflowing.

If he loved you
you would know it
not by words
but how he shows it.

Dear Woman:

He hit you again and
threatened your life
demanding that you'll
always be his wife.

He showed you the gun
and pulled out the knife
declaring he'll use them
if you give him strife.

You want to move on
but you well know
what might just happen
if you let him go.

It's hard to approach others
to help them see.
It seems no one takes you
seriously.

So you stay in fear
all by yourself
not being able to confide
in anyone else.

What do you do?
How can you break free?
Why won't this man
just let you be?

Know that God has not given you
the spirit of fear,
but power, a sound mind,
and strength to endure.

You must pray and believe
for the perfect time to leave.
Gain strength in numbers...
solicit others.

Confide in those with wisdom
like Counselors and Mothers.

Walk in your deliverance
because God set you free.

No weapon can prosper against you.
You have the victory!

There Is Strength In Numbers

Ride Or Die Chic

When your life is going up
or if it's going down
whatever the situation
she's always around.

You went to jail.
She paid your bail.
She brings a little Heaven,
when you go through hell.

You lost your job.
She uplifts you
letting you know
you can make it through.

All of your problems
she will understand
accepting and making you
a better man.

Sometimes you disagree
but it doesn't matter.
Her true intent
is to make you better.

She opens your eyes
to help you see
expressing her love unconditionally.

No matter the issue
by your side
she will stick.

Recognize you have found
a Ride or Die Chic.

Relationship Tip

For A Ride Or Die Chic

Relationship Tip:
Ladies,

Support your man in every situation.
If you don't sow seeds of support
in his time of trials and tribulations,
do not expect to reap a harvest of blessings
during his season of triumph and reward.

Declare this day,

I will serve and support you
through the ups and the downs,
the good and the bad,
and whether happy or sad.

Relationship Tip For
A Ride Or Die Chic

THE ART OF RECEIVING

Ladies:

The love of a man is like a butterfly.
If you hold your hand out and receive it,
it will come to you and land oh so gently.

But if you run after it and chase it,
in an attempt to catch it and grab it,
it will fly away never to return again.

The Art Of Receiving

SELF-PRESERVATION

When you have obtained self-preservation
you are careful of your friends and your relations.

You ensure that if you have a separation
it won't end up in dangerous confrontation.

The people in your life
should not bring you violent strife.
Self-preservation helps you know
of which people to let go.

Have wisdom in your choices.
Listen to those angry voices.
You must quickly cut them loose
or they'll become attached to you.

And fight you with their might
demanding that it's right
to stay into your life
regardless of the strife.

They are toxic to your soul
and don't mind destroying you.
If you don't allow them
to do what they want to.

Be mindful of my words
in case you haven't heard.
Don't call everybody "friend"
unless you know the beginning to the end.

Look Three Steps Ahead

Count The Cost Of Your Loss

Dear Man:

What you treat like trash

he'll treat like treasure.

What you feel is pain

he'll feel is pleasure.

So, before you drop her

make sure you measure

the loss you will gain

when someone else catch her.

Count The Cost Of Your Loss

Pay The Cost

Dear Single Man:

When you're not willing to pay the cost

all you'll be able to afford is the "knock off".

You don't get real for a steal...

Pay The Cost

LEARN TO MAKE HIM EARN

Dear Single Woman,

There's a learned lesson
in indiscretion
that I must
keep on stressing...

Do you say he is your man
claiming you're his biggest fan?

His name you always mention
trying to get his attention?

Liking all his posts
commenting the most?

All up in his face
letting him "pop up" at your place?

Sharing his statuses every day
and being an easy lay?

Although pursuing so hard
may seem like lots of fun.

You will not be so happy
when you find
that you're not "the one".

Let me give you a little wisdom
to ease your disappointment and strife.

A reasonable man will never have
a groupie as a wife.

Learn To Make Him Earn

The Best Is Yet To Come

Single Ladies:

God has anointed and appointed
you to a particular man.
Make sure that you are doing
all that you can.

God will give increase and favor
to that lucky guy
when he decides
to make you his bride.

So put yourself in a position
to produce the condition
that will bring all your dreams
into fruition...

The Best Is Yet To Come

YOUR BEST FRIEND

Your mate should be your best friend.

How can two have the same vision

unless eye to eye they see?

How can two walk together

unless they agree?

SHOW A LITTLE TACT

Single Ladies:

In regards to relationships,
God never blesses you
with a limited amount of tact.

But rather godly wisdom, prudence,
discretion, and an ability
to know how to act...

Show A Little Tact

Friends Till The End

Dear Friend:

There are some people in our lives
that will try to plant a seed
that you are insignificant
and someone I don't need.

That your acts of kindness
do not have impact in my life.
And your words of encouragement
do not end heaviness and strife.

Don't ever gain perspective
from those with unhealthy reason
who try to destroy what God has
ordained in this great season.

Your friendship is more valuable
than you'll ever know.
It pushes to a level
that will help all stretch and grow.

Have solace in my words
and be certain of one thing.

I appreciate the blessings
and the favor that
your friendship brings...

Friends Till The End

Supernatural Sistas

Ladies:

Be so supernaturally beautiful
that you will attract a man
that sees your amazing spirit
and cherishes your inner beauty.

You want to attract
the type of man
that looks beyond
shallow outward appearances.

A man that has the
depth to discern
a woman of character
and a woman of God.

Supernatural Sistas

THE ISSUES OF LIFE

Do you have a lot of baggage
that you cannot handle?

Internal issues that
produce so much scandal?

I know how you feel.
I've been there myself.

After continuous victimization
I could blame no one else.

Assaulted, and hated, and falsely accused,
battered, and beaten, and always abused.

I had to look within to see
what I was projecting...

To understand why predators
were always selecting...

Me, to be their victim
the one to perpetrate their pain on.

For it to stop
I had to get a gain on...

The issues at hand
and know from the start.

In order to be a victim
you must play the part.

The issues of life
flow from your heart.

Getting rid of those issues
is a form of art.

Stop mourning, stop crying,
throw away your tissues.

Recognize the part
that you played
in your issues.

Deal honestly and courageously
with the issues at hand.

And refuse to be a victim.
You must take a stand...

The Issues Of Life

THE POWER OF AGREEMENT

Singles:

Let me take you to your future
so I can help you see
what your world would be
if you don't agree.

Before you choose your husband
or before you choose your wife
be sure they can produce
agreement in your life.

Marriage is a platform for love
not a vehicle for strife.
It's environment should heal
like an ointment
not cut like a knife.

If you choose a mate that's not in agreement
your story won't go well.
You'll live a world of tension
 a life of living hell.

You're fighting and you're arguing
with negative energy.
You're tired and full of rage
because you don't agree.

And you feud, and you fight,
proving who is right.
Consuming each other's being
every day and every night.

No time for building a home
of purpose and legacy.
Your house is a battle zone
and your mate is the enemy.

Don't bother crying out to God.
Don't send it up there.
If you're not in agreement
He won't even answer your prayer.

So now you're left to yourselves
and with your own devices,
left with cuts, emotional bruises,
and all sorts of slices.

How can two walk together
unless they first agree?
How can they move forward
without the same philosophy?

Be mindful of my warning.
To my words
you must take heed.
Consider another partner
if you cannot agree...

The Power Of Agreement

DISCRETION

If you put everybody

in your business

that's where they'll be.

Learn when to share

and when to

keep it in prayer.

Discretion

WORD TO THE WISE

When you find you're in a sticky situation
you must determine what
has caused the complication.

Step back to assess your mess
and what caused you all the stress.

Take the time for some reflection
and proceed with some correction.

Go to the Lord and pray
to assist you along the way.

And make up your mind
not to do it the next time.

Although you cannot stop
all of life's aberrations.

You can reduce the times
of faulty implications.

Use wisdom and you'll know
that in time your life will grow
into a tree of continuous celebrations...

Word To The Wise

AN AMBIVALENT WOMAN

Dear Man:

There's a sticky situation
you don't want to see.

It's when a woman begins
to act ambivalently.

Whatever the issue,
she no longer cares.

Because she is not
emotionally "there".

You proved your point
and got it off your chest.

But now you are in
a much bigger mess.

You won the battle
but lost the war.

She now is headed
straight out that door.

It doesn't matter what you say.
She doesn't care what you do.

She's resolved in her heart
that she is through.

There's no more arguing.
There's no more commotion.

She has relinquished
all her emotion.

You won't hear her cry.
You won't see her fight.

No more staying awake
or worried all night.

If you encounter this behavior
be certain my friend

That she has determined
that it is the end...

85

GET YOUR ACT TOGETHER

Single Man:

I'm gonna tell you again
that you blew it.

But it ain't no since in telling you
cause you already knew it.

You're getting caught up in things
you know just ain't right.

Your Thirsty Side Chic's telling
what you did with her last night.

You're on your worst behavior
and you know it.

Mad at a Good Woman
because she got love and won't show it.

Not recognizing that
a Good Woman is smart.

Guarding her heart
before you tear it apart.

Now you're running around complaining
that a Good Woman is hard to find.

Not keeping in mind
that you're not her kind.

You wonder why
Thirsty Side Chics
with no tact
are all you attract?

It's simply because
you don't know how to act...

Get your act together
and do better...

Expose Your Own Heart If You Are Smart

Dear man:

Loving you is easy, cause you're beautiful...

But knowing when to trust you
and if she can release her heart to.

Making choices to change her life
when she doesn't feel really safe.

Not sure that your behavior
will leave her in a comfortable place.

Ensuring that your love is something
that will always stay.

A love that's strong enough
to make a suitable wife someday.

Ask yourself, what have I done
to ensure this woman can trust

That my words are more sincere
than just simple petty lust?

Have I done all that I can
to be a worthy man?

Have I broken communications
with the wrong relations?

Have I stepped up to the plate
to make sure that she feels safe?

Have I made the greatest investment
to be deserving of her trust and love

The kind that all others
could only dream of?

Only you, my dear male friend
can answer all those questions.

And you will be the one
that will teach others a lesson.

The lesson to stand by your word
to show this woman that true love is it.

Or a lesson that you're just a talker
with no intention to commit.

QUIT WASTING TIME
AND MAKE UP YOUR MIND

Dear Single Man:

She has taken most of her life
preparing to be the perfect wife.
She believed God and she prayed
that she would be a wife someday.

But you play and run around...
acting like a silly clown.
You waste your time on petty strife...
instead of searching for a wife.

You become intimate with the ones
that you know you'll never marry
and reject the type of woman
whose able to carry...

Your goals and all your dreams...
thinking you have plenty of time
to waste all of your days
and you won't make up your mind.

If you feel you're right and just
in the things that you are doing
and the relationships that you have
are really worth pursuing.

Then that good woman you rejected
while pursuing all of that
just made up in her mind that
she will leave you where you're at...

I Need New Shoes!

My Father gave me shoes
but I think they're too small.
Every step I take
they cause me to stall.

I should be grateful
but these shoes are so hateful!
I walk as I'm lame
because of the pain.

These shoes slow my pace.
I'm losing my race!
Every time they are worn
they produce a corn.

If I go to the market
and purchase new shoes,
I am pretty confident
this race I won't lose.

These shoes hurt so much!
I need a new pair!
Shoes not so tight
with less wear and less tear.

Shoes with support
to help me get there.
Shoes that will treat me
with love and great care.

These shoes hurt so bad
I don't know what to do!
I must go tell Dad...
I need new shoes!

Be Grateful

I try to figure out
why some people are sad
when all they need to do
is recognize what they have.

God's given them health
increase and wealth.
God's given them favor
and a life they can savor.

God's given them family,
friendship, and real love.
The kind they'll only receive
from Heaven above.

Then God will ask them
Why are you sad?
It seems to Me
that I should be mad.

I've given you all
there is to give
but the life I have given
you don't want to live.

What part do you play
in all of this sorrow?
Is it because you have
no faith in tomorrow?

If I gave you a promise
who's report would you believe?

If I said it in My Word,
who's word will you receive?"

The root of your sadness
is grown from the madness
that you simply refuse
to rejoice in God's gladness.

If you took the time to know
what others went through
you would be grateful for the gifts
God's given to you...

Be Grateful

Return Of The Mack

There's something in the air.
That still needs to be addressed.

Because women pursue so hard
men have learned to chase less...

Who can find a Virtuous Woman
for her price is worth more
than rubies and jewels.

And, in order to catch her.
You must have the tools.

You ought to be taught
on how a Virtuous Woman is caught.

The things that will please her
and the things that will not.

If you are willing to learn her,
she will teach you how to earn her.

Approach her, appease her,
please her, and tease her.

If you desire to obtain finer,
you must wine her and dine her.

Listen to her and love her.
Place no other woman above her.

But you have settled for less
instead of striving
for your best.

Allowing all of your fears
to increase your unhappiness.

You live in disappointment,
thirst, and slack,
insufficiency, hunger, and lack.

And it's simply because...
you have lost all your mack.

Return of the Mack.
The Mack Daddy
needs to come back.

To destroy all your fears.
Wipe away all your tears.

Give you what you desire.
Earn what you admire.

Approve you for love in life.
And move you towards
a Virtuous Wife...

95

VICTORIOUS LADY

Do you feel like a loser
because your relationship ended?
Are you angry and troubled
because you can't mend it?

Do you know why
your relationship failed?
Is it because of...
that no good male?

When you thought it was over
who did you blame?
Is it because...
that man is so lame?

Are you sure he's a liar?
Maybe he changed his mind.
After he discovered...
you weren't so kind.

Without confiding in you first
he started dating another.
Didn't wanna hear you screaming
and acting like his mother.

So he went on his way
without confrontation.
Didn't answer your calls.
Gave you no explanation.

Now you're bitter inside.
You demand it's his fault!

You swear he's been cheating.
Just didn't get caught!

You never took the time...
to step back
for a little reflection
to see why you're receiving...
so much rejection.

Before you go off on a tangent
and blame somebody else.
Take a deep breath and look...
within yourself.

Perhaps something inside
is causing you pain.
You must take it to Jesus.
Let Him explain.

He'll ease your mind.
He'll comfort your soul.
He'll make you beautiful inside.
And, He will make you whole.

And when you recognize
you're not a victim
then you will be free
to live life as Christ intended
as a Victorious Lady.

You will win when you are whole within.
Be made whole in your soul...

THE WRONG LIFE

I can't figure it out
no matter how hard I try.

The pain that I feel
makes me break down and cry.

This pain has manifested
from a series of choices.

My decision to listen
to the wrong voices.

So I did the wrong things
until I was taught.

I said the wrong words.
And I thought the wrong thoughts.

I picked the wrong places.
And I chose the wrong friends.

I didn't recognize
when it was the end.

I won the wrong battles.
And lost the wrong wars.

Opened the wrong windows.
Walked through the wrong doors.

I bought the wrong items.
And paid the wrong price.

Behaved like an idiot
when I should have been nice.

I married the wrong man.
He chose the wrong wife.

I went through a divorce
which cut like a knife.

Can't understand why
I have so much strife.

How did I end up
with...

The Wrong Life

Thoughts Are Things

For so many years
external battles I fought.

Until I finally recognized
my true enemy was my thought.

I no longer care what they say.
No longer care what they do.

All I care for is that...
I satisfy you.

My quest for perfection
in following Your direction

Will produce Your pleasure...
and continuous protection.

The thoughts that I think
will align with Your Word.

I don't care what is said
or what I have heard.

My decisions are based
on the way that You feel.

All other decisions
I determine to kill.

They say Thoughts Are Things
that will eventually bring...

The deepest manifestation
of what you're thinking.

Then if it is true
my thoughts of You

Will bring me to a place
of Heavenly grace...

And cause me to face...
a world of eternal blessings.

PERFECT LOVE CASTS OUT ALL FEAR

Dear Man:

You say you perfectly love her?
I will tell you if I must.

Perfect love without trust
is nothing but lust.

You don't listen to her perspectives.
You don't follow her directives.

You reject all her words
but receive what you "heard".

You don't ask the right questions.
You don't learn the right lessons.

You become angry at her
because she won't make the first move.

Closing your doors tight
unless she will prove...

That she will do anything
to reduce your ordained job.

Throwing her out of balance
and out of the divine order of God.

Women with discretion
will teach you a lesson.

They don't chase men.
They don't force friends.

They don't make the first move.
They have nothing to prove.

If you chase them
you may catch them.

If you don't
then you won't.

They have a keen understanding
of the Spiritual Laws of Attraction.

Recognizing God's plan for man
to pursue the first action.

Because the Spiritual Laws of Attraction
will let you know.

The one with the greatest investment
is the last one to let go.

She is a Woman of Wisdom.
Your love, she will ensure.

And, know that you'll respect and keep her
because you chose to endure.

There's something in the air
that needs to be addressed.

Because women pursue so hard
men have learned to chase less.

103

Stand up like a man
and take your position

Before you completely lose
what you have already been missing.

If there is a woman you perfectly love
what price will you pay

To make that particular woman
your beautiful wife some day?

You must learn to approach her first.
Believe God and pray

That the Holy Spirit will give you
the perfect words to say.

Take heed to my words
and attentively hear.

If you say you perfectly love her
then you should trust her...

Because...

Perfect Love Casts Out All Fear

Holiness In The Church

Single Ladies:

So you say you're in the church
and you learned to dress the part.

But it seems to me
that you haven't found
true holiness in your heart.

You dress like Driving Miss Daisy
but act like Sugg Avery.

You know the one on Color Purple
trying to be every man's lady?

Doing everything you can...
Running after every man...

Chasing...even if he ran...
Trying to catch a husband...

Unsuccessful, now you're stressed.
Begging God to please bless...

Your sin...and all of your mess...
While wearing that mammy made dress.

Running around acting deep with them.
Knowing if he asked
you would sleep with him.

As much as it's really worth.
We need to bring True Holiness
back to church.

DRESS THE PART

If you wanna be a wife someday
you must learn to dress the part.

Don't seduce him by dressing sexy.
Captivate his heart.

If you wanna be a wife someday
you must stimulate his mind.

Leave a little to the imagination
go get an education
and a husband you may find.

If you've gained a little weight
and your clothes are getting tight.

Gain the strength to let them go
because you well know
that they don't fit quite right.

I know just how you feel
after gaining thirty pounds myself.

I could see that it didn't fit me
and had to put it back on the shelf.

I'm gonna tell you a little secret
yet still a great reality.

No future husband of yours
wants every other man
viewing your sexuality.

So if you are voluptuous
and dressing sexy is your thing.

Delay the gratification
until the manifestation
of your diamond ring.

I know I sound old fashioned
for telling you to cover your chest.

But if you say...you wanna be a wife someday?
Be mindful of how you dress.

Dress The Part

FORWARD FOCUS FORWARD RESULTS

Dear Single Man:

In order to have success
and win in your life
you must choose the woman
who's the most appropriate wife.

Don't get afraid and fall backwards
to choose your ex.

You know...the one...
who mimics your next.

God shut down that season
for specific reason.

Defying God's command
is a form of treason.

If God told you to move forward.
Don't look back in your life.

Know your consequences.
Remember Lot's wife?

Your fear of the unknown
has caused you to settle.

Not recognizing
God's divine reason
to step in and meddle.

He's protecting you from disappointment,
insufficiency, and strife.

The feelings you'll feel
when you choose the wrong wife.

Be mindful of my words.
Know what you have to look towards

If you disobey God's command
and refuse to move forward...

Forward Focus Forward Results

LIFESTYLE COMPLICATIONS

SHORT REFLECTIONS OF LIFE SITUATIONS AND RELATIONSHIP COMPLICATIONS

I Want To Go To Disney!

As a little girl, I was told by my mom that my daddy was Santa Clause. I literally believed her! He was fat with a round belly, and jolly, with a beard and mustache.

Everything I asked for Christmas always came my way. I would make sure not to be naughty because Santa was my daddy! My birthday was three days after Christmas and I would ask for presents for my birthday and for Christmas. I knew that I would get anything I could imagine. Santa would make sure I had a happy birthday and a Merry Christmas.

On my sixth birthday, I jumped on my fat daddy's lap, hugged his big round pot belly, looked into his twinkling eyes, with much excitement, and asked him, "Will you take me to Disney?"

My dad replied, "Baby, you're too little to go to Disney right now and won't be able to ride anything. When you turn nine years old I will take you to Disney." I was sooooo excited! Every year on my birthday I would say, "It's almost time for Disney!" I could barely wait!

However, after my ninth birthday, a major tragedy happened to my daddy. A machine with molten brass blew up on my father at work and he sustained third degree burns over ninety five percent of his body!

My daddy was so loving and caring. Even though he was sick, he thought about me and told me that he hadn't forgotten about his promise to take me to Disney. He just would never be able to, because the burns on his body blistered and became very painful in hot weather.

As a little girl, I cried with tears streaming from my little eyes with such sadness and heartache. I cried because my daddy was very sick and I was afraid that he would die.

I also cried because I knew that I would never experience the fun and excitement that I wanted so dearly to experience with my fat daddy at Disney. I resolved within myself that my daddy and I would never go to Disney.

Twenty-five years after my dad's accident, in 2004, I asked my husband, "Will you take me to Disney?" My husband said, "Sure, make plans for us to go next year." I was sooooooo excited! I paid several hundreds of dollars for a timeshare with two suites for my husband, myself, and our six children to go to Disney. We would have so much fun!

Unfortunately, the following year, in 2005, I wasn't going to Disney at all, I was going through a divorce! The cares and vicissitudes of life became too heavy for our marriage, and it was unable to sustain any more injury and trauma.

Feeling a little disappointed, I went on my way to gain rest for my weary soul. I cried because I didn't know what would happen to me and my children after the divorce. I also cried because I knew that once again I was not going to Disney to enjoy the laughter and fun as a family.

A year later, I asked my kids, "Hey kids, why don't we go to Disney?" Two of my kids, responded, "Mom, don't you remember, we already went to Disney on a school trip? We don't want to go back to Disney." My other kids responded, "Mom, we're too old to go to Disney, we're teenagers now."

I thought, how can you ever be too old to go to Disney? I didn't want the timeshare to expire so I took my little timeshare and gave it to a young family at church. And guess what? They went to Disney!!!

It's been 40 years now, since I wanted to go to Disney. And you may be thinking to yourself, "Raynice, you're a grown woman, why don't you just go to Disney by yourself?" But you fail to realize, I don't want to go to Disney as a grown woman by myself. I don't want to walk the isles of Disney as a woman of experience and pain.

I want to capture the feeling that I had as an innocent little six year old girl, sitting on my fat daddy's lap, while laying my tiny head on his big pot belly, and looking into his jolly brown eyes, asking, "Will you take me to Disney?"

I want to erase all memories of disappointment, heartbreak, and trauma, as we run through the park, while being chased by security guards. I want to go to Disney!

I want to lick on a big round swirly colorful lollipop, eat pink and blue cotton candy, and take pictures with Mickey and Minnie. I want to go to Disney!

I want to wait in the lines for hours, without a care in the world, but to complain about the hot weather and sweltering heat, while drinking my cold bottled water. I want to go to Disney!

I want to delight my eyes on the majestic castles, talk to Donald Duck, and dress up like Cinderella. I want to go to Disney!

Will you take me to Disney?

MOTHER KNOWS BEST

One day, my youngest son, Bobby Joe, said to me, "Mama, you don't understand what we go through today as young people, because you were a nerd at our age. How can you tell us about something when you have never experienced it or gone through it yourself?"

I began to ponder on my son's question. Well, let's see...I skipped a grade in high school. I graduated Valedictorian, at the top of my class.

My first boyfriend became my husband. I never went out to parties or the club. I don't know how to dance. I don't smoke or drink, and I have never tried drugs a day in my life.

I completed a Bachelor's Degree, a four year degree, in only 3 years, with honors, while raising six kids, and being a wife, and meeting the needs of a husband.

My favorite subject is Math. I was a Middle School and High School Math Teacher for several years. Hmm...I guess I am a Bona Fide Nerd!!!!

However, my son, you don't have to necessarily have certain experiences to know that they aren't good for you. I don't need to gamble my money away, in order to figure out that gambling is a detriment to my financial health.

Some lessons in life are better learned without the pain of past experiences. There's no need to learn your lessons in strife, by having a hard knock life. Bobby Joe listen to your mother….. Mother Knows Best

LOVE AT FIRST SIGHT

And it came to pass, when Jacob saw Rachel...Rachel was beautiful and well favored. And Jacob loved Rachel; and said, I will serve thee seven years for Rachel thy younger daughter. Genesis 29:10-18

Ladies:

Is he loving you from a distance? There's a man out there who is watching you. He wants to know more about you. He sees your beautiful smile. He admires your character and how you carry yourself. Is he imagining a relationship with you from a distance?

He doesn't even know you personally, yet he loves you. He feels a connection with you, like you could be The One. He fantasizes about what it would be like to have a family with you. He feels in his heart that he wants to live the rest of his life with you.

There may be another more beautiful than you, younger than you, more successful than you, but it doesn't matter. It is you who have found favor in his eyes. He loves you and adores you. He chooses you.

Love At First Sight

Do Something Different

One day, I decided to go to a steakhouse for lunch. I am a meat and potatoes type of girl. I like food with a lot of sustenance. However, God told me to go to Olive Garden instead. He told me to do something different.

I left the Steak House's parking lot and drove next door to Olive Garden for soup and a salad. I was hungry and really wanted steak, but decided to be obedient to the voice of the Lord.

While at Olive Garden, I saw an old real estate business associate who's also a pilot. He just flew in from Brazil, and told me that he wasn't really doing real estate that much anymore.

I let him know that I specialized in Short Sales, where I negotiate with banks to allow my clients to sell their houses for less than what they owe, and I get banks to pay my clients as much as $15,000 to sell their houses that are "under water". We exchanged numbers and he left to go back out of the country.

Fifteen minutes later, after he left the restaurant, he gave me a call and told me that a client from Grand Rapids, Michigan just called him to ask him if he knew anyone who could help him sell his house, because he owes more than what it is worth. Immediately, my friend thought of me and sent the client to me. I sold that house and received over $6,000 in commissions!

When you are obedient to God, and you Do Something Different, God will open up the windows of Heaven and pour out a blessing that there is not room enough to receive. Break away from your comfort zone today and just do something different. Different actions produce different results in your life. Aren't you ready for a change? Go for it!

Do Something Different!

Make The First Move

One of my sons came to me a while ago and said, "Mom, I am unlucky in love. Only crazy girls ask me out on dates. I'm waiting on a quality girl to ask me out, but it seems like none ever do."

My son, your first issue is that quality ladies rarely ask men out on dates. They don't have to. They usually have many suitors that are vying for their love interest and their attention. Don't let that discourage you though. What God has for you, it is for you, but you must first ask for it. Did you know that you have not because you ask not?

If you want a quality lady, you may have to search long for her. She will be hard to find, because quality ladies do not advertise. You won't find her in any selfies, in the bathroom mirror, with all of her body parts hanging out, plastered all over Facebook and Instagram.

She is a lady of discretion, a lady that you would be proud to bring home to your mother. She is a godly woman. If she has children, her first priority will be for the well-being of her kids. She is resourceful and creative. She has goals in life.

Do not wait on her to find you. She never will, because she is not searching for you. She understands the dynamics of relationships. If you are not motivated enough to approach her, then how much more motivated will you be to maintain the relationship?

She understands that relationships take diligence and hard work.

Son, there are many fish in the sea. So much so, that you will have several fish flopping right in your boat, with no effort at all on your part. But this fish is the Big Catch. She will never flop in your boat.

In order to catch this fish, you must put on the bait, throw out the line, and strategically reel her in. If you want a quality girl, stop wasting your time waiting on her to come to you. You must...

Make The First Move

You Will Duplicate
What You Tolerate

One day, I was in a not so good mood. One of the Mothers of the church asked me, "Baby, what's wrong?" Well, I told her my sob story and my situation, thinking that she was going to have pity on me, and comfort me.

Instead, she firmly looked at me and said, "This problem that you are telling me, is not your problem. The real problem is....why did you accept that type behavior so long from another person in the first place? Now that's your problem!"

That's why I go to older women and Mothers for direction. They always have a word of wisdom. You see, Mother reminded me of a very valuable lesson that I seemed to ignore.

You train people how to treat you. You train them by what you tolerate. What you tolerate, you duplicate. What you duplicate, you adapt to. What you adapt to.... you have to.

You have to....because you have communicated that it is okay to continue the behavior, by your refusal to deal with it in the first place. By not expressing your displeasure in the situation, you have trained a person to believe that what they are doing is okay with you. They feel that you have to deal with it, because you chose not to address your dislike in the past.

In our everyday relationships, what are we tolerating? Do we see a pattern of behavior from people? I remember my first year of teaching. My students gave me turmoil. I couldn't understand why they were so good for other teachers, but would come to my classroom and cut up!

It was then that I learned this valuable lesson. I learned that the students acted out in my classroom, because I let them. I tolerated the behavior, and when, I finally did try to show some disciplinary measures, they became totally disrespectful, and would not receive it, because I had not required it in the first place.

The first day of the following school years would be exceptionally different. I put in place an expectation that I would not tolerate foolishness from students any longer. The students rose up to my expectations.

Soon after, my classes ran smoothly, and my kids were accelerating and getting the highest test scores in the whole school! I was awarded "Teacher of the Year" for consecutive years. I became respected and my students excelled. It was all based on what I did not tolerate.

What do you need to stop tolerating? Make a decision this day to refuse to allow other people's bad behavior to continue in your life. You will find that your life will be more enriched with peace and success. God bless!

TROUBLED WATER

Now there is at Jerusalem a pool, Bethesda. Great multitudes of impotent folk of blind, halt, withered, lay waiting for the moving water. For an angel went down at a certain season into the pool and troubled the water. Whosoever then first stepped in, was made whole. Now, a certain man was there with an infirmity for 38 years. Jesus asked him, "Will thou be made whole?" The impotent man answered him, "Sir, I have no man, when the water is troubled, to put me into the pool: but while I am coming, another steps down before me". John 5:1-7

In dating and relating, I know that men love the chase. But at some point, you must ask yourself, are you chasing or are you just running around in circles? A prudent and wise woman will allow you to chase for a while. And, she may even drop hints that she is interested. However, she can lead a horse to water, but she can't make him drink. She may even lay out a little salt and make that man thirsty, but it's ultimately up to him to make a decision to come forth and partake of the Pool of Bethesda.

Bethesda means House of Mercy. Has God brought mercy to your house, but you fail to partake of it? The lame man laid at the Pool of Bethesda for 38 years. He allowed others to partake of the water, but he wouldn't jump in.

He lied there, impotent, waiting for another man to place him in the pool. He failed to realize that another man would never give him the water, because, it is the nature of man to become competitive, when it comes to women.

Another man will try to partake of the water himself. If the impotent man would not make a decision to move forth, another man would see his lack of motivation, and take what was rightfully his.

Men, how many frogs have you allowed your soul mate to kiss, because you are not motivated to stop others from coming in and taking what is rightfully yours? Stop running around in circles and chasing your prize. It is your season. The angel has troubled the water. Go get your blessing! It's your time!

I Need A New Car!

When I left Michigan to go to California for a while, I gave my son, Bobby Joe, my Mercedes ML 320. I told Bobby Joe, "Don't let anybody else drive my car, but you, because the title and insurance is in my name. And, somebody is gonna get into an accident." The next day, Bobby Joe let somebody drive. Guess what? Yep, you guessed it, she got into an accident! I have no more patience with that vehicle...I Need A New Car!

Many folks know that my prophetic words come to pass quickly. When I speak, my words do not tarry long. And, I am not taking any more risks with that vehicle.

One day, I told two people that they were about to go to jail for a stupid reason. They simply had old traffic tickets that they refused to pay for over three years.

The next day, one was picked up by the police and went to jail. The following day, the second person was arrested.

That's why I refuse to be connected to a vehicle that everybody's driving. The risk and liability is too great. I Need A New Car!

These last few years, I've invested thousands of dollars in that vehicle. It was constantly breaking down. I had to pay top dollar for repairs, because of its name. It's a luxury car. Although it's been paid off for years, and I have no car note, it's more expensive to keep it. I declare! I'm not investing one more dime in that vehicle. I Need A New Car!!!

Since I've been in California, my brother drives me to all my business meetings and anywhere I want to go. Sometimes his schedule and his destination does not line up with where I'm trying to go. We will argue about whose plans are most important. I know...I'm riding in his vehicle, so my plans have to be laid to the side. That's why...I Need A New Car!

One of my brother's friends asked me, "Do you know how to drive, do you even have a license?" I told him that I know how to drive, and I have my license. I just don't know where I'm going sometimes. I need direction, so I don't get lost. And...I Need A New Car!

I've been driving for over 30 years. Although, I'm not the greatest driver, I've never been in an accident. Since I've had this particular vehicle, I've hit a parked car, a couple of fences, and some bushes.

I sometimes can't see that well. My vision may be a little "off" sometimes. After hitting a parked car, two fences, and running over some bushes, I determined that this vehicle brings me too much grief...I Need A New Car!

How many of you have been driving a vehicle that barely runs? You have to fight with it to get it started. Then it will move forward for a moment, only to cut off again.

It's difficult to reach your destination, when your vehicle is acting up. You must determine if it's worth the time and investment, or should you just trade it in for another vehicle. You could be very well driving the wrong vehicle. Declare this day...

I Need A New Car!!!

Empty Nest Syndrome

Several years ago I told my kids, "Mama Eagle is shaking the nest". Three kids were grown and gone, and I had five boys at home at the time. Then three more boys left and I had two eaglettes left at home. I twisted and turned the nest upside down, but could not get rid of these last two little eaglettes. After over two years, I finally gave up.

Then, my pastor preached a message about putting your grown kids out the house. He stated that it was the best thing his mama ever did when she put him and his brothers out. It sparked my interest a little. A week later, Bishop TD Jakes did a whole week series about shaking the nest. He even had a full nest on the pulpit!! After two or three witnesses, let every word be established, so I decided to do something about shaking my nest once again.

I bought my two eaglettes a nest of their own. I paid cash for it, so they would have no excuses about not being able to afford it. One eaglette cried out, "Mama please don't make me move with my brothers! They don't clean up after themselves!" The other eaglette cried out, " I'm not even 30 yet! Mama you're being selfish, you just want to live your life!"

Am I being selfish? Do you remember when your parents used to say, "This is gonna hurt me more than it hurts you?" Well it does, but I know that it's necessary for their growth. You see, my eaglettes were twenty and twenty one years old!! It was time for mama eagle to shake the nest!

We rehabbed their new nest and they moved in soon after. I felt a little sad and lost. For nearly 30 years, I always had little eaglettes running and playing around the house. There was always laughter, food, and fun. It was never a dull moment in our house.

After the eaglettes were all gone, the house was quiet and empty. There was no one for me to mother. It seemed as if my purpose had ended. Maybe my season of nuturing was no longer needed.

Now, I'm not sure I will know what to do. Perhaps I should buy a few cats and become the cat lady. What's a Mama Eagle to do?

Empty Nest Syndrome

GET WHAT YOU DESERVE

Do not arouse or awaken love until it so desires...
Song of Solomon 2:7

One of the largest causes of disagreement between a man and a woman in relationships is the time it takes for a man to make a decision to commit to love and to marry.

To a man, the decision of love and commitment to marriage is the most important decision of his life. He recognizes that the mate he chooses will affect his life and lifestyle in every capacity.

The mate he chooses will either fight with him, drain his energy needed for growth, and bring him down emotionally, spiritually, financially, and naturally.

Or she will encourage him, elevate him to higher heights, lessen the pains and the load in life, inspire him to be and do all that his heart desires, and cause favor and blessings to cover his life, all while adding increase spiritually, naturally, and financially.

The decision the man makes is a very serious one. Women must respect that decision. In order to get the love women desire and deserve, there are effective ways to approach the matter.

Never pressure a man to marry or commit to you. If you have to beg, force, and manipulate a man to get him, you will have to beg, force, and manipulate a man to keep him.

And, at some point he will get tired of your tactics and leave you. In addition, you will never be happy because he will never reciprocate the love that you give him or the love that you desire to have.

Always keep an upbeat and carefree attitude. The woman he chooses may not be the finest, richest, or youngest, but she will definitely be the woman who brings emotional balance and positive energy to his life

Keep your appearance impeccable. Men are visual creatures. To a man, the way you present yourself celebrates your love for him and your love for yourself. When you walk around looking unkempt, he will feel that you have no respect for yourself or for him, because to him, your appearance is a reflection of how you feel in the relationship.

Be your own person and do your own thing. You were called to be a "help meet" for your partner, however, your whole life should not revolve around him.

You should use balance and creativity to bring new energy and resources to the relationship. One can chase a thousand, and two can chase ten thousand. Be a multiplier, not just an addition.

And finally, if that man takes too long (however long that may be for you) to make the decision to commit to you and to marry you, have the strength and resolve to move on.

If he doesn't appreciate the gifts you bring to his table, take them home and give them to another.

Get What You Deserve

GET YOUR HOUSE IN ORDER

Let the older women teach the younger women to be sober, to love their husbands, to love their children, to be discreet, chaste, keepers at home. Titus 2:3-5

Ladies:

Are you a keeper of your home? In today's society, I know we have Women's Rights, and we can work as long and as hard as any man. We can make just as much money, but at the end of the day, are we keeping our homes?

You complain that he doesn't come home on time. Are you giving him a reason to? God has anointed and ordained us to have charge over the home.

Do you know that it is the woman that sets the "tone" in the home? What kind of music are you making? When he comes home, does he enter a sanctuary, a place of peace and tranquility, with kids in order, and the roast in the crock pot?

Or does he come home to a sink full of dirty dishes, no dinner, and a house full of nasty faced kids, with red Kool Aid stains around their mouths, screaming to the top of their lungs?

Ladies, we can bring home the bacon, and fry it up in a pan, but afterwards, let's make sure we clean up the mess.

Get Your House In Order

THE OBJECT OF HIS DESIRE

I am my beloved's and his desire is towards me.
Song of Solomon 7:10

Single Ladies:

Is his desire towards you? We as women, are emotional beings. We naturally have a strong desire towards the men that we are interested in.

A part of Eve's curse, after she ate of the apple, was that she would desire her husband, and he would have rule over her, or take advantage of that desire.

Thus, single ladies must ask, "Does the man I desire have the same desire for me?" If he does not desire you, should you waste your time? Desire is the glue that holds a relationship together. You may love a person, but if there is no desire for that person, you are no more than platonic friends.

How do you know that he desires you? Does he tell you? Does he give himself selflessly? Is he kind? Does he make an effort to give you his undivided attention? Are your thoughts, words, actions, and feelings important to him? Does he make an effort to please you?

Ladies, God has created you to be a wonderful gift. You were created for a purpose and with purpose. You are fearfully and wonderfully made. Be beautiful, be yourself, and be...

The Object Of His Desire

THIRSTY

And in that day, seven women shall take hold of one man saying, we will eat our own food and provide our own clothes; only let us be called by your name. Take away our disgrace!
Isaiah 4:1

Ladies:

Are you thirsty? My sons were having a conversation one day about thirsty girls. I felt a little old because I had no idea what thirsty meant. They laughed at my ignorance and proceeded to tell me.

A thirsty woman is a needy woman. She lacks discretion and will do whatever it takes to be accepted by a man. She will approach a man, and immediately let him know that she wants and desires him.

She requires no responsibility from him. He doesn't have to work. She will take care of him. He needs not to prove his love towards her. She will pay for dinner when they go out on dates. She will buy her own clothes as well as his.

She knows he has other women on the side, but she won't leave him. Instead, she will fight with his other women, arguing how she's his number one girl. She will allow anything. Please just don't leave her.

She is thirsty for love and wants him to supply her need. She has settled for mediocrity for the desire to be loved.

She does not know that Jesus loves her just as she is. Jesus will never leave her or forsake her.

Everyone who drinks this water will be thirsty again, but whoever drinks the water I give will never thirst. Indeed, the water I give will become a spring of water welling up to eternal life. John 4:13-14.

Try Jesus! You will never thirst again!

THE ESSENCE OF A WOMAN

Now it came to pass that a certain woman named Martha received Jesus into her house. And she had a sister named Mary, which also sat at Jesus' feet and heard His word. But Martha was burdened about much serving, and came to Him and said, Lord, dost thou not care that my sister hath left me to serve alone? Bid her therefore to help me..

And Jesus answered and said unto her, "Martha, Martha, thou art careful and troubled about many things: But one thing is needful: and Mary hath chosen that good part, which shall not be taken away from her." Luke 10:38-42

As women, we always talk about getting our Boaz. He is a biblical character that represents the epitome of the type of man that all single ladies desire to have.

He is a strong financial rock that loves us, and would protect us, and choose us, and place us into a place of honor. He is an authoritative figure that all others look up to. His money and power makes him the perfect selection to any woman's dreams.

I beg to differ with you girls. There is a man that is much more attractive than Boaz. He will love you selflessly. He would die for you. And, the earth is His, the fullness thereof, the world, and they that dwell therein.

His name is JESUS. There is revelation knowledge in this passage that would teach any woman to have the man of her dreams, if she could only see.

Ladies, in regards to relating to men, have you chosen that good part? There was something about Mary that attracted the attention of the greatest man that ever lived, Jesus. What was it about Mary, that had Jesus defending her, even though her sister Martha did everything for Jesus.

Martha invited Jesus to her house. Martha cooked and slaved to make Jesus comfortable. Why were Martha's ways rejected, but Mary's ways received? Men require the chase. When you do everything for a man, you cause him to lose interest in you.

In the initial stages of a relationship, he needs to have the opportunity to work for you, you should never work hard to get a man to approve of you. That means that you should not be calling, texting, and asking men out for dates. You should not be buying him gifts, food, clothes, or other items that would cause him to feel obligated to be nice to you.

There is time to nurture him, once he puts a ring on your finger. Acting like a wife, before you are one, will ensure that you won't be one for a very long time. Whatever you do, do not work to please a man or gain his attention.

What shall we do? There is a way that will attract a man to you. It is your ESSENCE. The way you carry yourself, your serene and quiet spirit, your attitude of calm, even when he's acting up, your ability to redirect his emotional turmoil and cause peace to heal his heart.

Your ability to simply enjoy his presence and to accept him as he is, not nag him, in an attempt to change him.

You shouldn't be acting like his mama. He doesn't need your advice of how to live his life. He's done well without you thus far.

It's been said that communication is about 5% of what you say, and 95% of nonverbal cues. Be that woman of confidence, solitude, and grace in his life. Don't try to work so hard at convincing him that you are the one. Be the one!

THE BUSINESS OF LOVE

Every relationship should have some business qualities to succeed:

1. Get your goals in place: Where do you want to be as a couple in 5, 10, 15, and 20 years from now? Create a vision and plan out your lives together.

2. Get your systems in place: Work your systems through dates, love, laughter, and responsibilities. After awhile, your systematic approach will automatically run smoothly. You will be doing all the successful things, on purpose, to make your relationship work.

3. Get your money in place: Map out your financial blueprint. Determine to get out of debt, increase investments, gain more financial knowledge, and plan the financial future for your children and your children's children.

God wants you to prosper in every aspect of your life, spiritually, naturally, and financially. Determine this day that you will work as a team. You are business partners, who compensate for each other's weaknesses, while building a foundation of love, faith, wealth, and happiness.

What's His Make Up

A couple of days ago, I was going through my make up bag, looking for a particular item. The problem was, I didn't know what I was looking for.

I was in a hurry, so I became very frustrated. Internally, I was anxious, nervous, feeling needy, upset, and really impatient, because I needed the item, but I didn't even know what it was. Finally, I took a step back, took a deep breath, and thought to myself, "What do I want? What am I looking for?"

Immediately, a peace came over me. I was looking for my brown eye shadow! At that point, among all the chaos in my make up bag, I pointed out my eyeshadow effortlessly, with no stress and no pressure at all...

Ladies: Men are like makeup. They are there to cover you, compliment you, and to enhance your beautiful characteristics. Do you know what it is you want in a man? Do you know what type of make up the man should have, to make you, your most beautiful self? If you are feeling, anxious, needy, nervous, and impatient, perhaps you should take a step back. Write down 10 characteristics you would like to have in a man, and let God bring that man to you. God will bring you the perfect match.

Write the vision, and make it plain on tablets, so that he may run who reads it. For the vision is yet for an appointed time; But at the end it will speak, and it will not lie. Though it tarries, wait for it. Because it will surely come, it will not tarry.   Habakkuk 2:2-3.

God's got a blessing with your name on it! Write it down and watch God bring it to pass!

SILLY WOMEN

This know also that in the last days perilous times shall come. For men shall be lovers of their own selves, proud, without natural affection, false accusers, despisers of those that are good...lovers of pleasure more than lovers of God. Having a form of godliness, but denying the power thereof. For of this sort are they which creep into houses, and lead captive silly women laden with sins, led.away with divers lusts... II Timothy 3:1-6

Ladies:

Are you silly? Silly is defined as a person that lacks good judgment or common sense, a foolish person. Whenever the Bible defines a silly woman, it is in reference to the type of men that she allows in her life or her home. As single women, we must be mindful of how we relate to men and the types of relationships we put ourselves in, especially if we have children.

Some women don't understand that if they lack good judgment in the types of men they choose to relate with, they are creating a consistent pattern that could destroy their lives and the lives of their children.

This pattern or way of doing things will ensure that she remains single for the rest of her life, because no quality man will take her as a wife.

She is wasting precious time because she has settled for anything that comes her way. She has begun a vicious circle of a quantity of men over quality men. There are some basic rules to follow that ensure that you do not become a silly woman.

1. Never allow men to come to your house on the 1st date. Your home is your covering. If you determine that he is a nut, you don't want him knowing where you live.

2. Never sleep with a man on the first date. Sex is a very intimate matter. Once a woman sleeps with a man, she bonds emotionally with him. However, men don't think that way.

If you sleep with him too soon, he feels the chase is over. If at all possible, wait until marriage, where you know that he's emotionally connected to you, because he chose you. If you're too weak, please use wisdom and discretion either way.

3. Listen to that inner voice that tells you "NO"! It is the Holy Spirit trying to protect you from the wrong one. The Holy Spirit is a keeper. He will keep you and preserve you for Mr. Right, if you let Him.

4. If you're dating someone for awhile, make sure your relationship is solid before introducing them to your kids. Your kids shouldn't see you with a number of different men. Don't let your good be evil spoken of. Appearances are everything.

5. Never allow men to spend the night and sleep with you around your children. You should never display your sexuality around your kids with a man that is not your husband. You must model respectful behavior. Many kids don't respect their mothers today, because their mothers failed to respect themselves around their kids, in regards to men.

If you have been a silly woman in the past, you can now repent and turn from your wicked ways. God wants to bless you, but you must hold up the standard. May this day, you make a decision to live right, so the right one can enter your life.

LET IT GO

But if the unbelieving depart, let them depart. A brother or a sister is not under bondage in such cases: but God hath called us to peace... 1 Corinthians 7:15

In the scripture above, Paul the Apostle was referring to an unsaved marriage partner leaving their Christian partner for believing in Christ. However, there is revelation knowledge in this text that can be used for everyday dating and relating.

Have you ever been in a relationship where your partner no longer believes in you? Have they lost faith in who you are and what you can bring to their life? Usually, when a person leaves a relationship, they are leaving based upon some unresolved need within themselves that has not been met through the person they deemed responsible for meeting that need.

It can often cause the rejected party to become bitter, hurt, unloved, bewildered, stressed, angry, and with an abundance of negative emotions growing inside. In the midst of all the emotional turmoil, you must ask yourself how should you respond to rejection?

You claim you were in love, and now your loved one left you. My question to you is, what's love got to do with it? You see, how you love someone and how you feel for someone has absolutely nothing to do with how you should respond to a break up. If the unbeliever departs, let them. They do not have the faith to believe that you can supply their needs. I proclaim this day;

do not cry, do not beg, do not plead with them to stay with you. You are only making the situation worse. You must let them go. God has called you to be at peace in the midst of your inner emotional storm.

Sometimes, people need space, and an opportunity to step back to reflect if what they are doing is right for them, especially when it's a life changing decision. You must respect that. Give them their space. If they come back to you, and you make a decision to take them back, then your relationship will be stronger. If they don't come back, then God has someone better suited and tailor made for your specific needs.

God knows what you need, even before you ask. Believe God this day. God has called you to peace. Don't call, don't text, don't email, don't contact. Peace! Be still...

LET IT GO

The Common Denominator

You can blame everyone around you for the situations and circumstances that arise in your life, but at what point are you going to realize that the only common denominator of the same situations and circumstances that you are in is you?

If everybody is mistreating you, could it possibly be that there's something within you that subconsciously attracts and accepts mistreatment? Take responsibility for the circumstances that arrive in your life. Know that every situation is a learning experience, meant to catapult you to your next season.

All things happen for a reason and for a season. Trust God and ask Him to give you the understanding of every trial and tribulation. God is righteous and He is faithful. He will reveal to you, and He will see you through.

Frenemies

Dear Friends:

A humble and contrite heart, God will not despise. Lay humbly before the Lord and watch Him lay a table before you in the presence of your enemies. God is causing you to experience pain, because He desires to slough off the dross of your frenemies.

As a result of your tribulation, He's making their motives clear and their actions known, by the words that are proceeding from their mouths. He knows your giving heart, and He is protecting you from the unqualified ones who will come to attach themselves to the blessings that are on your life.

The blessing God has for you is so big!!! He wants to ensure that when it overflows, it will only fall on those who truly have your heart and your well being in mind.

When you're finished going through. Watch who comes to you. If they didn't have your back, you'll know what to do...

POTIPHAR'S WIFE

Joseph was a godly young man who prospered in everything he did. He was thrown in a pit and sold as a slave to Potiphar. The Anointing on Joseph's life gave him favor with Potiphar. Potiphar gave Joseph full access to anything in his house, except his wife of course.

Unfortunately, the Anointing on Joseph's life was very attractive. As a result, Potiphar's Wife asked him to sleep with her. Joseph rejected her advances. Therefore, Potipher's Wife retaliated by using her power and influence to falsely accuse Joseph and have him placed in prison for over 10 years of his life.

Recognizing the Spirit of Potiphar's Wife:

Potiphar's Wife can show up in either a male or female. She is not human. She is a spirit and, a way of doing things. Potiphar's Wife will ask you to participate in drugs, an illicit affair, an unwanted relationship, giving money, or anything else you choose not to do. You know you have encountered Potiphar's Wife when she begins to destroy your credibility and reputation and place you in a prison of false accusations and attacks after you reject her.

How to deal with Potiphar's Wife:

1) Don't try to convince people that Potiphar's Wife is lying on you. The more you attempt to explain that she is a liar and an Accuser of the Brethren, the less people will believe you.

2) Maintain a positive attitude of patience in prison. Joseph never complained about Potipher's Wife lying on him. He remained positive and patient while waiting on his deliverance.

3) Forgive Potiphar's Wife and let go of all bitterness. Joseph did not become bitter. He just continued to use his gifts and allowed the Anointing to work in his life while in prison.

In the end, God blessed Joseph greatly and he became second in command in all the nation. Joseph knew that all things worked together for the good of those who love the Lord and who are called according to His purpose. Don't let Potiphar's Wife distract you or discourage you. Be healed and keep the faith.

God Bless You!

Dating And Relating

I've heard a lot about dating and Christian singles lately. I would like to expound on the subject and bring wisdom to the issue. I've read a lot regarding the subject, and find, that many Christians feel that Single Christians should not date, and that they should only court.

I disagree with that rationale. I also believe that single women are strongly hurt by this mindset. Many Christians base the "No Dating" and "Only Courting" rule from the perspective that in Biblical times, Christians did not date. However, they fail to put the issue into perspective, that Christians rarely chose their own spouses as well.

In our day and time, and in our culture, we choose our own spouses and therefore, must make an informed and experienced decision on who our spouse will be. I cringe, when I hear single women saying that the next man that goes out with them can only court them and not date them. Those women are ensuring that they will be single for many years to come.

The reason why is the expectation that they place on any man that they immediately meet. They have, "The Lord Told Me, You're My Husband" mentality in regards to relating to men. They immediately want to attach to a man and have him commit to them and treat them like his wife, before they have earned his trust and love. This is a sure way to scare any man off, the moment he

149

senses that mentality. Men are hunters, and they can smell neediness and unrealistic expectations a mile away.

Ladies, remember if the Lord told you that he's your husband, God will manage to let him know as well. Let that man figure it out for himself. Remember, you are a queen. And, if he's too slow to figure it out, you don't want to submit to anyone who doesn't have enough sense to know that he's your leader and king.

Dating is the interviewing stage of a relationship. It is a safety net that catches you before you fall in love with the wrong person. It is necessary before going to the next level, which is courtship. And it is necessary for both parties.

As a woman, you may discover that the man you're dating doesn't want kids, and you want five. Maybe, he won't be the best fit for your future. Or, he may discover some idiosyncrasy about you that is a deal breaker. It's better to discover these things out, before becoming too emotionally involved.

I find that dating, in and of itself, is not bad. What's bad is how people are dating. Dating should never be used by men as a tool to get sex, or used by women as a tool to get a free meal. It is a time of reflecting and objectively looking at the other person, to see if they are someone who you could possibly live the rest of your life with.

You should set boundaries and parameters to dating. In addition, you should set internal time limits. As women, if a man wants to date indefinitely, you should never give him an ultimatum. Instead, give him space.

Leave him alone, and choose to date new people who have better respect for your time. As men, if you know that she's not the one, don't continue to prolong a dating relationship with her, because you're lonely or don't have better options at the time.

Move on as quickly as possible, so that you can focus on another who could be a better fit. You will also lessen the drama of expectation when you break it off quickly. The longer a woman is in a dating relationship, the more she expects that you are taking it to the next level, which is a normal expectation, depending on how long the relationship has persisted.

Overall, as singles, if we choose to adhere to godly principles during our dating season, we can have a very rewarding single life where new experiences are developed and new people are met. Whether they become our spouses or not, we learn that we can successfully relate to the opposite sex, therefore, strengthening our interpersonal skills.

Dating And Relating

Passion In The Pursuit

Pursuit displays passion. If he does not ask you, he doesn't deserve you. If he doesn't deserve you, you don't want to. You don't want to be with a man that does not give you full assurance that his desire is towards you.

Don't waste a bit of emotional energy on him. Don't bind yourself to an "emotional affair" or "fantasy relationship", making excuses that he's just too shy, going through some changes, having some issues right now, etc. Don't stop living your fabulous life. Date men who pursue you.

A man that does not ask you for a date or a relationship, etc., does not want to. You should never waste your time or emotional energy, waiting on a man to ask you, because you think he likes you. He can give you an array of excuses of why he doesn't want to at this time. It doesn't matter.

There's someone out there that he's asking, with no excuses at all, and, it's not you. Move on with your life. You are not an option. You are a choice. Choose men who choose you. There's...

Passion In The Pursuit

ARE YOU AN ASSET OR A LIABILITY?

Are you a financial asset or liability? A few years ago, my house burned down. I said to the Lord, "I built this house fifteen years ago. Even though it's almost 5000 square feet, with 24 foot ceilings, 6 foot palladium windows throughout, 6 bedrooms, and 4 baths, I will build the next one bigger and better!"

The Lord asked me how much did it cost to run my house. I said about $6,000 a month. Then He said, "When you get married, will you be a financial asset or liability?"

The market is sluggish right now, and you will want to move with your husband when you get one. But he will have to think, "She has almost $75,000 a year she pays out in debt. We can't sell her house, because she owes more than it's worth. Every month we don't get a renter, I must dump $6,000 dollars into a non performing liability, or simply become financially devastated, because we can't afford two mortgages. Is it cheaper NOT to keep her? When I count the cost, will I realize that I didn't win, but I lost?"

So I asked, "What shall I do Lord?" He told me that I will live beneath my means, and I will pay cash for my houses, or have very little debt, until my husband finds me. I will give my husband the gift and blessing of "Raynice", not the curse of debt.

Are you an emotional asset or liability? The other day the Lord asked me, "What do you see?" I said that I see a woman, who has been engaged to a man for more than a year. But throughout her engagement, every time they come to a disagreement, she goes out, and finds new lovers to sleep with.

She is a strange woman, who causes men to commit adultery with her, for Your Word considers an engagement as a covenant of marriage. She preys on men by telling them that she loves them and she will give them peac. But, they don't know that sudden destruction is near.

When she gets angry with them, she goes back to her fiancee, flaunts that she's getting married, and brags how she wins. She mocks those and accuses them of stalking her. But her fiancee, being a man of wisdom, walks away from her again, when he sees her manipulative ways.

Then, she will immediately go back after those she seduced before, with a sad heart. She quickly attaches herself to them, acting like she is in love. She thinks "love and peace" is a feeling. She doesn't recognize that they have so many more attributes than that. "love and peace" is a spiritual decision.

She lacks the concept of covenant, commitment, character, and self control. Men of spiritual discernment and emotional strength will see her adulterous ways and run.

She preys on men who are emotionally broken and hurt, who desire love and peace. She gives them a false sense of peace and love by satisfying their fleshly desires for a season and speaking words as smooth as a honey comb. They do not consider that her strange ways will lead them to hell and poverty. Proverbs 5:1-13, 6:24-29

She must repent, be still, and understand that her ways are not pleasing to God. He loves her, but He hates her ways. If she does not change, and when men become emotionally whole, they will ask themselves, "Is she an emotional asset or liability? When I count the cost, will I find that I didn't win, but lost?"

Are you a spiritual asset or liability? As I spoke of sticky situations, many great men came up against me. They wanted to shut my mouth, because I spoke of things they did in the dark. Most of the time, I didn't even know it.

I did my best not to offend, but with every series I taught and every situation I spoke of, they became angrier, more bitter, and more hateful toward me. They called me weird, a witch, a weed, a wolf, and whatever wicked thing that could come from their mouths.

They did not understand that Your Spirit is just as offended with them as they live in their flesh. Their flesh grieves Your Holy Spirit. Do they not recognize that I am simply a woman who is Your mouthpiece?

Do I have the strength of a man to fight them? Do they not know that as much as their flesh wants me to shut up, my flesh desires not to speak of such things?

Are not my enemies' flesh and my flesh both in agreement? But, it is Your Spirit that causes enmity between our flesh, causing me to speak of matters that do not concern me.

Yet there was one, that is as great as those men, a Defender of the Defenseless, who rose up and spoke on my behalf. They took every conversation, and argument I had with You Lord, and they spoke prophetically, and verbatim, the words that came out of my mouth, concerning these matters.

But now, they are disheartened with me, not understanding why I would remain in that environment. They don't understand that I can't move from my assignment until You release me.

I tell you what I will do. I have guarded my heart for such a time as this. I'm not going to say another thing that doesn't concern me. If Your people want to live in their flesh, let them. What do their deeds have to do with me?

And the Lord said, "Raynice, concerning your spiritual self, are you a spiritual asset or a spiritual liability? When I count the cost, will I discover souls you didn't win, because of your disobedience, but souls you have lost?"

Are You An Asset Or Are You A Liability?

I Don't Wanna Be Right

I want to honor two of my loved ones who lost their lives. I don't understand why God allows some situations in life. Sometimes we lose loved ones. There is a time to live and a time to die. It is the Circle of Life. It simply hurts when it hits home. Death of a loved one is never easy. It raises all kinds of questions from those of us who experienced it.

Our reaction to death can be very hard and emotional. It causes us to question God sometimes. But we must understand that all things work together for the good of those who love God. And as sure as we live and breathe, someone we love will die. It does not reduce the sting of death, knowing that we will experience it. We can only live the best life possible and let our loved ones know that we love them while they're able to receive it.

I have been a prophet for twenty years. In that twenty years, I warned three people of death, if they did not obey the Lord. Two of those three people died. They were my loved ones and I grieved greatly.

I will present to you my thoughts at the time, by writing through poetic expression. I want you to know that I understand the feeling of loss of a loved one. And, I too, do not understand why God had to take the ones I loved. I do know that God is just, righteous, and fair. However, the human desire to never lose a loved one is real. Sometimes...I don't wanna be right.

Dear Loved Ones:

You know a prophet by if their words come to pass. Sometimes I have words of increase. Sometimes I have words of warning. Mark my words...

Prophets edify the Body of Christ. We edify the spirit, not the flesh. Prophets that only give good words are known as false in the Bible.

One day, I prayed for a pregnant lady. She was pregnant with a breech baby. Her doctor told her that her umbilical cord was tied around the baby's neck and the baby would strangle and die once he attempted to deliver. The doctor feared they would cut through the umbilical cord, so they could not give her a Cesarean-Section.

She did not disclose her pregnancy situation to me. However, I walked up to her placed my hand on her belly and told her about her situation. I informed her that she was carrying a son. But I had a different outcome and response from the doctor.

Without knowing, I told her that her baby had her umbilicol chord wrapped around his neck and he was a breech baby boy. However, he would live and he was turning around in her stomach. Soon after, the umbilical cord released from her baby's neck. The next week, she delivered a healthy baby boy. God turned that breech situation around for the pregnant lady and her baby. Her baby lived.

God is turning that breech situation around in your life as well. You shall live and not die and proclaim the salvation of the Lord. God is turning that situation around in your favor.

There were many prophetic specialists in the Bible. Jeremiah was the weeping prophet. John The Baptist paved the way for Jesus. Hosea had an adulterous wife that he used to compare our adulterous behavior towards God. John The Revelator prophesied the end times. Elijah had a heavy mantle. Prophets are sent for special assignments.

I have been sent to help you recognize your situation. There is wisdom in understanding why you're in the situations that you are in. I warned of death three times in twenty years of my prophetic ministry.

The first person died in five years. That was the time limit I warned God would give. I begged the person to leave a certain town and a certain apartment complex, or they would regret it within five years. I screamed, leave now! Something terrible is gonna happen! You are going to remember my words and wish you had listened! The person cursed me and wouldn't speak to me again.

The fifth year, they were found naked, in a pool of blood, strangled, and stabbed to death in that apartment building. I cried for my loved one, because I was right.

The second person died within five months after not obeying the word of God. I cried out. Stay away from those people and those places! They are gonna have you shot and killed! Please don't go back! The person told me that I didn't understand. He said that those people and that environment was like family to him. Five months later, those people led him into a place and a situation where he was shot to death. I cried for my loved one, because I was right.

In both incidents, the murders were publicized, dramatized, and scandalized. Their murders were all over television and the media. In both cases, God gave one person five years, and the other, five months. Five is the number of grace. Don't let grace go. The third person has not experienced death. The third person has time and the grace to obey the Word of the Lord.

I speak life and life more abundantly! May I never have to speak a word of death again. May we live and see the salvation of the Lord.

When my loved ones died, I was grieved in my spirit and I cried out. I told God if warning His people of death is right, let me be wrong...I don't wanna be right!

I told God that I will no longer warn His people. I wash my hands of their situations. God responded by saying that the hands that I wash will be bathed in the blood of those I refuse to warn...Blood on my hands.

Life and Death are in the power of the tongue. I proclaim to you all....Choose Life!!! So that you and your seed may live! I'm not trying to control or manipulate you. I simply want to show you your options. May you use wisdom in your choices. For there is a way that seems right to man, but the end thereof is death.

Today, many prophets are afraid that their words won't come to pass when they speak. I'm afraid that my words will come to pass...I don't wanna be right.

Twenty years ago, my uncle asked me, "How do you know that you're a true prophet of God?" I smiled and bragged, "Because 98% of my words come to pass swiftly." My uncle then asked me, "What about the other 2%?" I smiled and said, "Oh uncle, they're coming to pass soon, they're still just tarrying." But twenty years later...I Don't Wanna Be Right.

What Have I Done To You?

Transparent Prophetic Prayer:

Lord, when I stayed, I was accused of being Jezebel and a Manipulator. When I left, I was accused of being Disloyal and Inconsistent. When I visited, I was accused of being a Distraction that causes Division and Discord. They will accuse me, no matter what I do...so I will ask them, "What have I done to you?"

I never personally spoken a negative word to my accusers in my life! Neither have I ever done anything to my accusers! In fact, all I've ever spoken is blessings and increase over their lives, when I speak of them or speak to them...so tell me, what have I done to you?

There is a spiritual ringing in my ears. I hear my name being spoken across this nation, like I've done something to hurt, harm, and destroy. Even though I speak well of their names, my name and integrity is being annihilated by them.

Several women are being confided in about how horrible I am. I hear all of them saying the same thing to my accusers, "She ain't right! Use discernment! Let her go!"

How can someone let go of....what they never possessed? How can someone release what has never been in their hands? What have I done to you people?

Men are being confided in, concerning me, across this country. I hear my accusers saying, "I have no peace around her. "I'm not at peace!" You have had no personal contact with me, so why are you so troubled with me? Why are you not at peace?

Have my prophetic words taken away your peace to live comfortably in sin? Have my words troubled your heart? I insist! Tell me. What have I done to you? Are my prophetic poems of living holy, with prudence and discretion, not sleeping around, allowing Jesus to quench our thirst, making a decision to get married, than to live in fornication. Are these simply my own sinister concepts, with no Biblical backing?

Are my poems untruthful concepts, with no godly merit? Please tell me...the Lord has not revealed it unto me.... what have I done to you?

So, I pray:

Lord, cause us to recognize our true enemy. God, You are not the author of confusion. Take away our root of bitterness and offense toward each other. Heal our souls from the aggravation of the enemy.

Don't allow Satan to crawl into the minds of your people, and speak to their imaginations, by telling them that I'm out to destroy them.

Give them peace concerning me, so they can live an effective Christian walk and move forward in the things You called them to do. Cause them to hold on to no bitterness concerning me. And let them know that I'm not out to destroy them, but I pray that all is well with them.

And Lord, let my Sisters and Brothers in Christ know that I love them and I'm not mad at them or against them. When I speak prophetic poems, I don't want to speak against their deeds, I don't even know their deeds, but I must proclaim what You told me to say, or risk Your wrath.

I don't want to hurt anyone. I don't want to cause pain. I know my prophetic poems are strong, and I try to hold them in, but it's like Fire, shut up in my bones, and I can't hold back. Lord, speak to their spirits and let them know that I love them, and that I wish above all, that they prosper and be in health, even as their souls prosper.

PS:

As a prophet, I wish I could speak all good, happy, positive words to you. I wish I could tell you that God is pleased with our hearts and our behavior. But, He's not. And especially my heart! He's shown me first, the error of my ways.

I need you Lord. I need a heart that runs after Your heart... so that I will not cause pain, and I will recognize...What I have done to your people...amen

I Am Not Your Enemy. I love all of you, those who hate and despise me, with no cause...as well as those who love me and celebrate me. So, tell me...

What Have I Done To You?

Bad Affiliations Ruin
Your Reputation

Several years ago, as a young woman, I longed for acceptance and to fit in. But, all I encountered was rejection, sticky situations, and false accusations. I did not understand. Neither did I recognize that my poor choices of associations caused my relational tribulations. After much heartache, pain, and sorrow, God gave me a revelation. He instructed me to study and monitor my affiliations.

Mark those who think negatively about you, who speak ill of you, are offended by who you are, can't handle your presence, and lack toleration. Join those who bring out the best in you, love you, receive your gifts, think highly of you, and consider your life a celebration. And always remember, Wrong Affiliations Ruin Your Reputation. So, know those who labor among you.

AND LIFESTYLE COMPLICATIONS

Messages Of Wisdom From My Friend

Dear Raynice,

In life we always learn. Sometimes we learn to forget.

We all remember the game, "Show Me Yours and I Will Show You Mine".

When you step out first in faith as a man or woman, it's "truth or dare".

As we have gotten older and wiser, we are not easily taken by words alone.

In my world, it's called prima fascia evidence. In your world, it's called proof.

Trust is one thing verified, and validation is another.

I'll take a trip to investigate the possibility, but I know what cards to hold and unfold.

With some of us, a smile and pretty butt is just not enough. Men and women who have a little, ain't interested in buying a pig and a poke.

Sight unseen. When you haven't put anything in it, you get nothing out of it.

The truth is, everything that glitters ain't gold.

My grandmothers were field girls. My mom was a field girl. Ruth and Naomi were field women.

Once you have been married in a significant marriage, and that person has gone and passed away, you're simply not just interested in anything or anyone selfish in their ways or wants.

You know what love is? Not real. But true love is as the Lord says.

As He said, "Pressed down and shaken together!" It shall be given to you!!

Sincerely,

Steven Givhan Phd

A Call To Repentance

That if you confess with your mouth the Lord Jesus and believe in your heart that God has raised Him from the dead, you will be saved........ Romans 10:9

It is my primary life's mission to direct others to be healed and whole in their souls. The most important step to wholeness in your soul is to become aligned with the source of all healing. We have had an opportunity to recognize situations in our lives that may not have been optimal.

There have been some good days and bad days. However, if we can connect to the root of all healing, we will perpetually win in life. For what is it to gain the whole world, but lose your soul?

Man is appointed but a season on earth, and our time may be full of sorrow. There is a Person who can wipe away all your tears. His name is Jesus. And if you confess His Name today, you can have everlasting life. Please repeat this little prayer after me...

Heavenly Father, You are great and worthy. I believe that Jesus is Your Son, and He died on the cross for our sins, so that we may have eternal life. I confess today, that Jesus is Lord, and believe in my heart, that God raised Him from the dead. In Jesus Name I pray, Amen....

Congratulations!!!! You are saved! You have been redeemed! Welcome to your new journey of peace and happiness, regardless of the situation!

Now go and find a church home that you can connect to, so that you can be fed the precious Word of God.

God Bless You!

Enter Into A Life Changing Journey Of Soul Restoration And Spiritual Growth

Raynice L. Starr

Raynice L. Starr will bring healing to every situation of your life. The beginning of healing is clarity. You must know why you're going through trials and tribulations in order to effectively address them. Raynice's unique skill sets will successfully assist you in addressing every situation that approaches your life. You will begin to live a healthy whole lifestyle. You will be able to conquer every condition that held you hostage. For a complete list of Raynice Starr's books, workbooks, products, and other resources, please visit:

WWW.RAYNICESTARR.COM

Raynice Starr will deliver a powerful and life changing seminar or workshop on a variety of subjects such as health, love, spiritual growth, finances, and beauty. She is well rounded and specializes in many topics. For more information on scheduling speaking engagements, seminars, and workshops, feel free to contact: bookingraynicestarr@gmail.com.

You Can Have Clarity In Every Situation You Encounter. You Don't Have To Go Through Your Situation Alone!

There are several products available to help you work out situations. Raynice Starr will work with you to assist you in first, recognizing your issue. Next, she will help you find the answer you have been diligently searching for to get through your situation. Last, Raynice will inspire you and support you in your journey to wholeness. You don't have to live through trials and tribulations not knowing which way to go, or what to do to end your struggle. There is a right way and a wrong way to respond in every situation. Discover the tools you need to succeed and win in life.

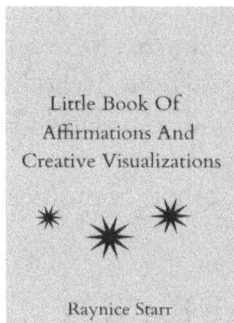

Little Book Of Affirmations And Creative Visualizations

Inspire You To Be The Higher You Lifestyle Planner

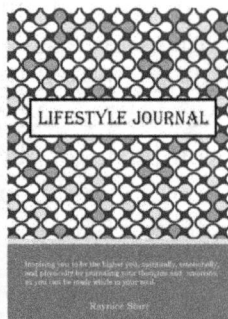

Inspire You To Be The Higher You Lifestyle Journal

AVAILABLE AT RAYNICESTARR.COM

Be Made Whole From
The Situations Of Life.
Be Made Whole In Your Soul

Sticky Situaltions And Lifestyle Complications Workbook is a great addition to Sticky Situations And Lifestyle Complications, A Poetic Prelude. After reading issues in life that may affect your well-being, feel free to work on recognizng your specific situation, and bring clarity in your life. Then, take the time to work out solutions to every situation you encounter. You can be made whole in your soul. Raynice Starr will help you apply effective principles to difficult situations so you can achieve your goals and desires.

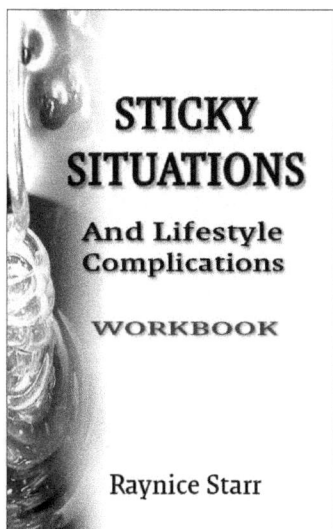

STICKY SITUATIONS
And Lifestyle Complications
WORKBOOK

Raynice Starr

AVAILABLE AT RAYNICESTARR.COM

www.ingramcontent.com/pod-product-compliance
Lightning Source LLC
LaVergne TN
LVHW051236080426
835513LV00016B/1623